COUNTRY FRUITS & FLOWERS

CLAIRE WEBB

MEREHURST

To my sister, Alex – without her help I would never have finished the work on this book –
and to my parents for all their help and continued support.

Published in 1995 by Merehurst Limited, Ferry House, 51-57 Lacy Road, Putney, London SW15 1PR

ISBN 1-85391-401-0

Managing Editor Bridget Jones
Edited by Donna Wood
Designed by Jo Tapper
Photography by Ian O'Leary
Colour separation by Global Colour, Malaysia
Printed by Wing King Tong, Hong Kong

Acknowledgements
The author and publisher would like to thank the following for their assistance:
Anniversary House (Cake Decorations) Ltd., Unit 16, Elliott Road, West Howe Industrial Estate, Bournemouth, BH11 8LZ;
A.P. Cutters, Treelands, Hillside Road, Bleadon, Weston-Super-Mare, Avon, BS24 OAA;
Cake Art Ltd., Venture Way, Crown Estate, Priorswood, Taunton, TA2 8DE;
Claire's Sugar Craft, Norfolk House Yard, St Nicholas Street, Diss, Norfolk, IP22 3LB;
Guy, Paul & Co. Ltd., Unit B4, Foundary Way, Little End Road, Eaton Socon, Cambridge PE19 3JH;
House of Cakes, 18 Meadow Close, Woodley, Stockport, Cheshire, SK6 1QZ;
Squires Kitchen, Squires House, 3 Waverley Lane, Farnham, Surrey, GU9 8BB.

NOTES ON USING THE RECIPES
For all recipes, quantities are given in metric, Imperial and cup measurements. Follow one set of measures only as they are not interchangeable. Standard 5ml teaspoons (tsp) and 15ml tablespoons (tbsp) are used. Australian readers, whose tablespoons measure 20ml, should adjust quantities accordingly. All spoon measures are assumed to be level unless otherwise stated.
Eggs are a standard size 3 (medium) unless otherwise stated.

CONTENTS

INTRODUCTION

Cake decorating is an absorbing hobby, a rewarding occupation and one which I have enjoyed for some years. I started by decorating a friend's wedding cake, then progressed to entering sugarcraft competitions, displaying work at exhibitions, teaching and, for the last three years, running a specialist shop for other sugarcraft enthusiasts.

The particular subject which I enjoy is wild flowers as they provide such a wide range of colours, textures and environments on which to focus sugarcraft studies. For this book, I have also looked at the variety of fruits which naturally complement the flowers. The seasons and the natural settings for the plants often provide the starting point for creating a design and this aspect of studying the living plants before moving on to modelling them in sugar is an important, and pleasurable, part of my work.

The satisfaction of watching enthusiasm and skill grow in others when teaching is good reason for bringing together information in a book. I hope you will feel inspired as you look through this book and that you will enjoy working from it as much as I have enjoyed writing it. It has been an experience for me and one which I hope you will share as you discover the details in the step-by-step photographs and written instructions.

TIPS FOR SUCCESS

The following are some of the techniques which I have used throughout the book for individual projects.

SUGARPASTE SUPPORTS In the teardrop-shaped cakes I have used small amounts of sugarpaste to support the flowers and find it a very successful method. Decide on the position for the flowers and set the sugarpaste in place with a small amount of royal icing. Leave the paste to set for about 24 hours. If you try to arrange the flowers immediately, they will fall over.

DEEP-COLOURED FLOWERS AND LEAVES When making very dark flowers and leaves, such as poppies, it is best to work with sugarpaste three to four shades lighter than the finished result you actually require. When the flowers or leaves are dry, a deep-coloured dusting powder (petal dust/blossom tint) can be brushed over them. The flowers or leaves can then be steamed. If necessary, a second layer of powder can be applied once the paste is completely dry and the flowers or leaves steamed again.

PAINTING When painting on an item which is to be removed from the cake and kept rather than eaten, for example a plaque, you may find it easier to transfer the image or words with a pencil rather than scribing them.

Liquid food colouring, paste or powder may be used. Mixing the colour with a little clear alcohol, such as gin or vodka, makes it dry quickly and this prevents the colours from running. Always ensure that the surface is dry before painting on it as any moisture will cause the picture to lose definition.

FLOWER PASTE Use a small amount of cornflour (cornstarch) on your hands if the paste is sticking to them.

If flower paste begins to lose its elasticity, knead a small amount of gum tragacanth into it and leave it for 30 – 60 minutes.

If the paste begins to crumble, knead it with a little white vegetable fat (shortening) or egg white.

EQUIPMENT

Much of the equipment mentioned in this book may already be owned by many cake decorators, but there are certain items that are specific to the designs illustrated in this book. All cutters referred to have been drawn, see individual projects and page 70, so templates can be traced if necessary. Florists' tape is used most of the time – I find the paper-type is best. Floristry wire is available either covered or uncovered – it is useful to have both types. The higher the number, the thinner the wire becomes; heavier wire, such as 24-gauge, is generally used for larger leaves and flowers. Stamens, again used widely, can be made if necessary, see page 9, but some commercial ones are also required. Flat dusting brushes, although not essential, are very useful as they allow more control over where the powder goes. Veiners are a must, see page 12.

USEFUL EQUIPMENT FOR FLOWER-MAKING INCLUDES: edible food colouring, paste and liquid; dusting powder (petal dust/blossom tint); assorted floristry wires; non-stick board and rolling pin; selection of modelling tools; various cutters; florists' tape; selection of paintbrushes; tweezers, pliers and scissors; selection of veiners; dowel rod; cotton (thread); stamens; flower paste; confectioners' glaze; egg white or gum arabic solution; foam pad/sponge; cocktail sticks (toothpicks); oasis.

ROYAL ICING

❖

This royal icing is made using albumen powder.

*440g (14 oz/2½ cups) icing
(confectioners') sugar
67g (2¼ oz/⅓ cup) reconstituted albumen
1 tsp glycerine*

● Place 315g (10 oz/1¾ cups) of the icing sugar in the bowl of an electric food mixer. Add the reconstituted albumen, then beat on level 5 for 4 – 5 minutes. Add the rest of the icing sugar and beat for another 6 – 7 minutes on level 3. Beat in the glycerine for 1 minute.

● Transfer to an airtight container and leave overnight. Beat lightly with a spatula before use.

RECONSTITUTING ALBUMEN POWDER

❖

● Pour 625ml (1 pint/2½ cups) cold water into a grease-free bowl. Add 90g (3 oz/½ cup) albumen powder and whisk well. Cover and place in the refrigerator overnight.

● Sterilize a piece of clean, fine, undyed silk in boiling water and wring out. Strain the albumen through the silk, then store it in an airtight container in the refrigerator. Use within 2½ weeks.

GUM ARABIC

❖

● Use one part of gum arabic to three parts of boiling water. Place the gum arabic into a small, sterilized, heatproof jar. Add 3 tsp boiling water, stir and leave to dissolve.

● This solution can be used instead of egg white when assembling and sticking the separate pieces of flowers.

● For a stronger 'glue' break off a small piece of flower paste and mix it to a paste with the gum arabic solution. This will make a strong, tacky adhesive suitable for repairs as well as for assembling items.

FLOWER PASTE

❖

*500g (1 lb/3 cups) icing (confectioners') sugar
3 tsp gum tragacanth
2½ tsp powdered gelatine
5 tsp warm water
2 tsp liquid glucose
15ml (1 tbsp) white vegetable fat (shortening)
1 large egg white*

● Put the icing (confectioners') sugar into a heatproof bowl. Mix in the gum tragacanth. Place in the oven on a very low setting to warm.

● Place the water in a heatproof bowl. Stir in the liquid glucose and vegetable fat, then sprinkle the gelatine over. Place over a pan of hot water and heat through, stirring occasionally after the first 5 minutes, until the ingredients have dissolved.

● Warm the beater attachment for an electric food mixer. Transfer the sugar to the mixer bowl. Add the dissolved ingredients and the egg white. With the mixer on its lowest speed, beat until the mixture starts to come away from the sides of the bowl in strings.

● Knead the paste together into a smooth ball. Store the paste in a polythene bag in an airtight container in the refrigerator. Leave for 24 hours before use.

BASIC FLOWER-MAKING TECHNIQUES

❖

Cupping, veining and frilling or softening edges are the three basic techniques that are used in flower making. Reproducing pollen effect and making stamens are also common techniques for many flowers. Other techniques are used for specific blooms and they are shown as applicable throughout the book.

POLLEN Replica pollen is manufactured commercially or it can be made by colouring either corn meal or semolina mixed with dusting powder (petal dust/blossom tint).

STAMENS Some flowers need many stamens. To make these, take some cotton in the colour required and wrap it around two fingers approximately 50 times to make a loop. Thread pieces of thin wire through the ends of this loop and twist them to secure the pieces of cotton. Cut the cotton loop in half to make two bunches of stamens. Attach the stamens to a longer piece of wire and secure them with florists' tape. Trim the cotton ends to the required length. If a centre is required, splay the cotton leaving a gap in the centre, then place a tiny ball of green flower paste in the middle. Brush the ends of the cotton with egg white and dip them into textured powder.

EXPERT ADVICE

≈

When softening the edges of the leaves and petals, first turn them over so the underside is uppermost. Less definition will be lost from the front of the leaf or petal.

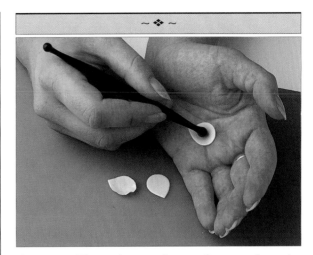

~ ❖ ~

CUPPING Place the petal on a foam pad or the palm of your hand. Using a dogbone tool or ball tool, rub the centre of the petal in a circular movement to form a slight cup shape.

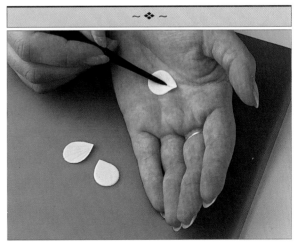

~ ❖ ~

VEINING This is used for marking leaves or petals. Place the leaf or petal on a foam pad or the palm of your hand. Using a dresden tool, make lines from the base of the leaf or petal towards the top edges.

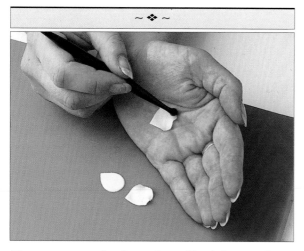

FRILLING or softening edges. Used for petals or leaves. Place the petal or leaf on a foam pad or the palm of your hand. Use a dogbone or ball tool and run it back and forth on the edge of the petal or leaf. This will cause the paste to frill slightly and it will soften the cut edge.

PEBBLES These are easy to make and very effective. Just take a piece of flower paste and lightly knead some black or brown colour into it, leaving it part-mixed to give a marbled effect. Roll small pieces of the paste into pebble shapes. Leave to dry. Pebbles can also be made with small pieces of leftover sugarpaste that has started to harden.

CROSS-SECTION OF A FLOWER

The main parts of a flower are petals, stamens, ovaries, sepals and stigma. Normally the petal is the largest and most eyecatching part of the plant. Underneath are the sepals, which form the calyx. Inside the flower are the stamens – the male part of the flower where the pollen is produced. The female part of the flower is the ovaries, each one having one or more pollen-receptive stigmas.

Flowers are usually constructed with both male and female parts, but this is not always the case. Plants such as the mistletoe have separate male and female flowers on different plants.

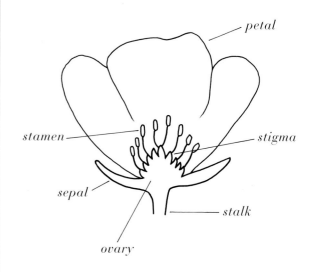

LEAVES

❖

Leaves are as important as flowers. Without good foliage the overall effect of the arrangement is lost, so take the time necessary to achieve good detail and colour.

In this book I have used leaves in all of the designs. The basic technique for making them is the same; the colour, shape and veins tell them apart. Although a wide range of leaf cutters and veiners is now available, you will not find them for all the leaves used throughout the book. Instead all the shapes required have been illustrated, so that templates can be made from card. As long as you cut carefully around the template, a nice clean edge will be achieved. I usually use green or cream flower paste as a base colour dependent on which leaf is made.

BASIC METHOD OF MAKING LEAVES Take a piece of flower paste in the colour required. Roll it out thinly on a non-stick board, lightly greased if necessary, leaving a thin ridge in the centre. Cut out the leaf shape required. Vein the leaf, see page 12, with either a fresh leaf or a commercial veiner. If holes are wanted in the leaves, make these at this stage with a pin or scribing tool.

Dip the appropriate wire into some egg white. Hold the leaf between your index finger and thumb and insert the wire into the ridge. Gently smooth the edge of the leaf with a dogbone tool; twist the leaf slightly to give it a more natural look. Leave to dry overnight.

If card templates are being used to make the leaves, use the same method as before. Line up the template centre with the ridge, cut out with a scalpel, vein and gently soften the edges. Insert wire; leave to dry.

Double-sided tape can be stuck to the card. The leaf, vein-side up, is then attached to this and the template can be cut out. This allows both the correct vein and the correct shape to be obtained at once.

For linear leaves, such as bluebell and daffodil, take a piece of green paste; roll into a sausage. Take an appropriate piece of wire, dip it into some egg white and pull it through the centre of the paste, lengthways. Place the paste on a non-stick board; flatten it slightly. Roll the paste either side of the wire with a dowel rod and cut out the shape required with a pair of scissors. Vein down the centre of the leaf and soften the edges using a dogbone tool.

To make flat leaves, for example violet and wild strawberry, roll the paste without a ridge, cut out the leaf shape, vein and soften the edges. Take a piece of wire, in the appropriate gauge, and bend a small section at one end, at a right angle. Cut a small patch of paste, brush some egg white over this and place it over the wire to attach it to the back of the leaf. Hang the leaf upside down to dry.

Colour the leaf with dusting powder (petal dust/blossom tint); use brown in the areas that have holes. Use a flat brush and work from the outside towards the centre. Glaze as necessary, see page 13.

If making dead or dried leaves, dust all over with assorted shades of brown powder. Some of the red and yellow shades can be used if desired. Remember dead leaves have a tendency to be more curled up than fresh ones, so this can be emphasized when shaping.

Tiny leaves, such as birdsfoot trefoil, are made by rolling the paste very thin and without a ridge. Scientific wire is attached to the back with egg white.

VEINING

There are many veiners now available on the market and most good sugarcraft shops stock them. However, they can quite easily be made using non-toxic modelling clay or, alternatively, by using real leaves and petals, backed with lightweight card.

REAL LEAVES Pick a fresh leaf which is undamaged and has a good vein pattern. Give it a quick rinse and dry it well. Roll some flower paste as necessary. Lightly grease the underside of the fresh leaf with white vegetable fat (shortening). Place the greased side of the leaf on the sugarpaste, press down lightly, then cut around the edge with a scalpel. Remove the leaf to reveal the veins in the flower paste leaf.

COMMERCIAL VEINERS These are mainly available in plastic or rubber, and are either single- or double-sided. With a single-sided veiner, after a leaf shape has been cut out, place the veiner on top, apply gentle pressure with a piece of foam sponge and remove. If you are using double-sided veiners, place the paste leaf shape between the two veiners and squeeze them together before removing.

Lightly dust the single-sided veiner with a little cornflour (cornstarch) and press on the thinly rolled paste. A cornflour dusting bag may be used to gently press the paste against the veiner. Peel the paste off the veiner, then trim the edges with fine scissors.

When using a double-sided veiner, the paste is laid on the bottom half of the veiner and the top half pressed in position. When the veiner is opened the paste can be gently peeled off. Dust both sides of the veiner with cornflour (cornstarch) to prevent the paste from sticking.

Home-made veiners can be made using fresh leaves as shown here. The leaves should be undamaged, clean and dry. Stick them to a piece of thin card using double-sided sticky tape so that the side with most prominent veins is uppermost. Cut around the leaf shapes with a pair of sharp scissors.

GLAZING

There are three main ways of glazing leaves and petals.

FAT Once colouring with dusting powder (petal dust/blossom tint) has been completed, a fat glaze can be added. Melt a little white vegetable fat (shortening) on a saucer over a small saucepan of hot water. Then paint it over the leaf or petal using a paintbrush.

STEAM When the leaves or petals are dusted with colour, gently pass them through the steam of a kettle. This will give the paste a slight sheen and help to prevent tiny fragments of dusting powder (petal dust/blossom tint) from falling on the surface of the cake.

CONFECTIONERS' GLAZE This can either be used full strength or at half strength. The latter gives a less-bright shine. To make the half-strength glaze, place 3 tsp glaze in a small wide-necked jar. Gradually add 2 tsp vodka, shaking well between each addition to prevent the varnish from becoming spongy in texture.

Basic Leaf Types

trifoliate

pinnate

linear

lobed

lanceolate

palmate

TARA

20 x 15cm (8 x 6 in) oval cake
apricot glaze
1.25kg (2.5 lb) marzipan (almond paste)
1.25kg (2.5 lb) sugarpaste
clear alcohol (gin or vodka)
Royal Icing, see page 8
a selection of food colourings
EQUIPMENT
28 x 23cm (11 x 9 in) oval cake board
no. 42 piping tube (tip)
small paintbrushes
1m (1 yd) of 15mm (⅝ in) wide ribbon to
trim board
FLOWERS
5 acorns, see page 17
18 oak leaves, see page 18
2 conkers, see page 19
10 horse chestnut leaves, see page 18
2 oak apples, see page 16

● Using the template on page 16, make a sugarpaste plaque. Leave to dry. Trace the picture of the dog on page 16 and transfer the picture to the plaque. Paint with food colourings.

● Brush the cake with apricot glaze and cover with marzipan (almond paste). Allow to dry. Coat the board with sugarpaste and set aside.

● Cut an oval shape from a piece of card as for the plaque. Place the cardboard template on the marzipan and scribe around it to mark the position for the plaque, then trace this onto a piece of greaseproof paper (parchment) cut to fit the top of the cake.

● Brush the marzipan with clear alcohol, taking care not to dampen the marked area for the plaque. Coat the cake with sugarpaste.

Place the cardboard template on the cake and line it up with the mark on the greaseproof paper. Using a scalpel, cut around the template. Carefully lift out the cut oval of sugarpaste.

● Set the finished plaque in position on the cake and gently run your fingertips around the cut edge of the sugarpaste to smooth it right up to the edge of the plaque. Leave the cake to dry.

● When the sugarpaste is firm, place the cake on the board. Pipe a line of royal icing around the join between the plaque and sugarpaste, then smooth it neatly with your fingertips.

● Using a no. 42 piping tube (tip), pipe a snail trail around the base of the cake. Using the template on page 16, trace and paint the scene on the side of the cake using food colourings.

● Make the acorns, conkers and leaves and arrange them on the cake. When you are happy with the arrangement, attach the pieces with royal icing. Attach the ribbon to the board using double-sided tape.

EXPERT ADVICE
≈

When making acorns, to make the cup more easily, a real acorn cup can be used to make a mould. Push it into some non-toxic modelling clay to make an impression. When the mould is dry, flower paste can be pushed into the mould, then hollowed out using a dogbone tool.

MAKING OAK APPLES

To make an oak apple, take a marble-sized piece of brown flower paste and roll it into a ball. Make a small hole in the ball with a cocktail stick. Make a hook in the end of a piece of 26-gauge wire and dip it into egg white, then insert it into the bottom of the ball of paste. Continue making the oak apples, pushing their stems into a piece of polystyrene as you complete them. Leave to dry. Dust the oak apples with dark brown dusting powder (petal dust/blossom tint). Steam them and join them together in pairs or in threes, using brown tape, with the little hole showing at the front.

Tara Plaque

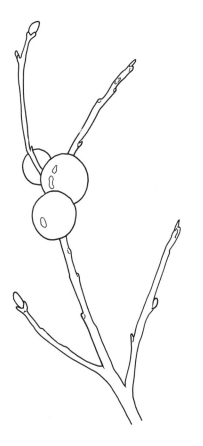

Side Design

~ 1 ~

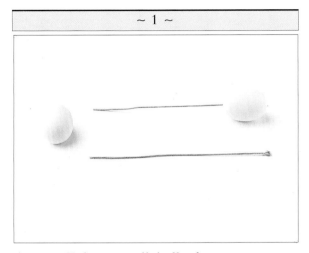

ACORNS *Take a small ball of cream or green flower paste; roll it into an egg shape. Take a piece of 26-gauge hooked wire, dip the wire into egg white and insert into the base of the paste. Place a small cream stamen at the top. Leave to dry.*

~ 2 ~

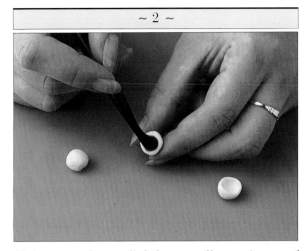

Take another slightly smaller piece of sugarpaste, push the small end of a dogbone tool into the middle of the ball and hollow out to make a shallow cup. Thin the edges of the cup.

~ 3 ~

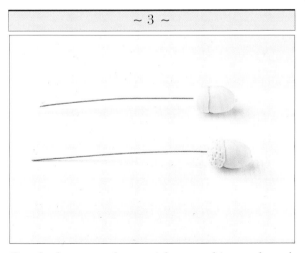

Brush the acorn base with egg white and push the cup on underneath it. Gently mould the cup to fit the nut neatly. Texture the cup with a nutmeg grater or a similar fine grater blade. Leave to dry.

~ 4 ~

When dry, dust the acorn and the cup with dusting powder (petal dust/blossom tint), making the cup slightly darker. Varnish the nut only with half-strength confectioners' glaze; leave to dry. Arrange acorns in pairs with leaves surrounding them, see page 18.

OAK LEAVES AND
HORSE CHESTNUT LEAVES

❖

Leaves, such as horse chestnut and oak, tend to show quite a range of colour variation. The best way to achieve individual results is to experiment with different colours. Always try to use a selection of real leaves as a guide. For example, take several colours of dusting powder (petal dust/blossom tint), such as brown, rust and yellow, and dust the leaves with small sections of colour. Then lightly brush over the leaves again to blend the colours. Sometimes a little black powder around the edges helps to define the shape of the leaves. Follow the notes on pages 11 – 13 and use the templates shown here for making the leaves. Tape the chestnut leaves together in groups of five for this cake.

EXPERT ADVICE

≈

When you have finished dusting the leaves pass them through the steam of a kettle. This helps to set the colour and also helps to stop tiny fragments of powder falling onto the surface of the finished cake.

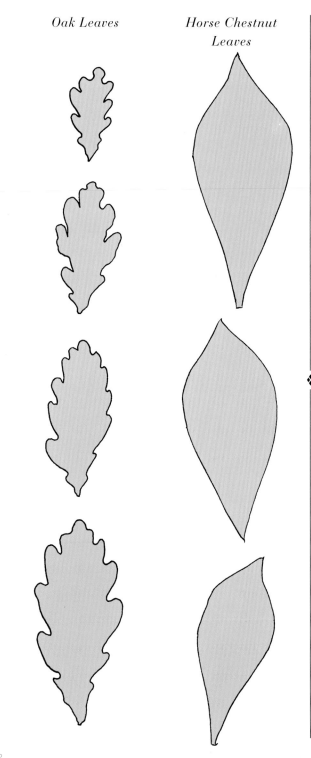

Oak Leaves

Horse Chestnut Leaves

~ 1 ~

CONKERS *Colour some flower paste with terracotta paste colour. Break off a small piece of paste to the size required and roll into a conker shape – rounded and slightly flattened on top. Leave to dry.*

~ 2 ~

Dust the conker with brown powder, leaving a small circle uncoloured on top. Take some champagne dusting powder (petal dust/ blossom tint), mix it to a paste with a little alcohol and paint the circle. When dry, varnish the brown part with confectioners' glaze.

~ 3 ~

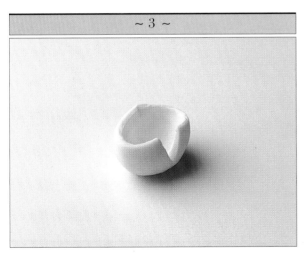

To make the shell, take a piece of flower paste and roll into a ball. Hollow out with a ball tool, then put the conker inside for a moment to make sure it is the correct size. Cut a 'V' shape in the side of the shell and trim the top to make the edge square. Leave to dry.

~ 4 ~

Make the spikes by rolling tiny sausages of paste with pointed ends. Cut these in half and secure to the shell with egg white or gum arabic solution. Leave to dry. When dry, dust outside with brown and green and inside with a pale rusty colour. Pass through steam.

HARVEST CAKE

25cm (10 in) teardrop cake
apricot glaze
1kg (2 lb) marzipan (almond paste)
1.25kg (2.5 lb) sugarpaste
clear alcohol (gin or vodka)
Royal Icing, see page 8
a selection of food colourings
EQUIPMENT
25 x 30cm (10 x 12 in) oval cake board
no. 42 piping tube (tip)
small paintbrushes
1m (1 yd) of 3mm (⅛ in) wide ribbon to
trim cake
1m (1 yd) of 15mm (⅝ in) wide ribbon to
trim board
FLOWERS
2 stems of oats, see page 22
3 poppies, see pages 22 – 23
3 poppy buds, see right
8 poppy leaves, see pages 11 – 13

● Brush the cake with apricot glaze and cover with marzipan (almond paste). Allow to dry. Coat the board with sugarpaste; set to one side. Brush the cake with clear alcohol; coat with sugarpaste. When the icing is firm, transfer the cake to the board. For this cake, as the design is painted directly on top, the sugarpaste needs to be left to dry for at least a week.

● Trace the mouse picture on page 70 onto a piece of greaseproof paper (parchment). Place on the cake and scribe the outline gently into the sugarpaste. Paint in the details with food colourings. Leave to dry.

● Pipe a snail trail of icing around the base of the cake using a no. 42 piping tube (tip). Place two lines of thin ribbon above this, securing them with royal icing.

● Make the oats and poppies. Take a piece of sugarpaste and make into a small mound. Stick this on the board in the concave curve of the cake and use as a base in which to arrange the flowers. Hide the sugarpaste by covering it with pebbles. Attach the ribbon to the board using double-sided tape.

THE POPPY ARRANGEMENT

MAKING BUDS Tape two pieces of 26-gauge wire together and make a hook in one end. Take a medium piece of green sugarpaste and roll it into an oval bud shape. Dip the hooked end of the wire into egg white, then place the bud on it. Use a craft knife to cut a single, shallow line lengthways down each side of the bud. Prick tiny holes in the surface of the bud and leave to dry. When dry, paint red dusting powder (petal dust/blossom tint) down the lines on the sides of the bud – this gives the effect of the bud just opening. Steam the bud. Leave to dry.

LEAVES Use the templates on page 22 to make the leaves and follow the instructions on pages 11– 13.

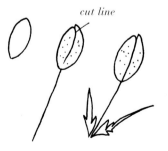

cut line

Poppy Bud

MAKING OATS

Colour some flower paste very pale cream. Cut several 5cm (2 in) lengths of 36-gauge scientific wire. Hook one end of a piece of wire. Take a tiny ball of paste, dip the wire into egg white, then push it into the ball of paste. To make the husk, roll a small piece of paste into a cone approximately 1cm (½ in) long, making sure the pointed end is very fine. Cut up the length of the paste. Open out the cut and thin down either side on your index finger, making sure the paste is very fine. Vein the husk on a corn leaf veiner. Brush a little egg white on the inside of the husk, then push the wire with the small ball of paste through the centre. Leave to dry.

cut

open up cut and thin down edges

Tape the husks together using white tape. Make several stems and join them at different levels. Dust with cream dusting powder (petal dust/blossom tint), making the stem a darker shade than the husks. Steam over a kettle.

To make the grassy piece of the oats, cut two or three pieces of 33-gauge white wire. Roll some cream paste into a sausage and pull the wire lengthways through the middle. Flatten the paste with a palette knife, then roll it on either side of the wire until very thin and almost translucent. Cut the paste into a blade shape with the wire down the middle. Transfer the blade of paste to a foam mat and vein down the middle with a dresden tool. Arrange in a natural-looking position and leave to dry. Dust with cream powder and tape to the oat stem, keeping the lengths about 1cm (½ in) apart.

POPPIES

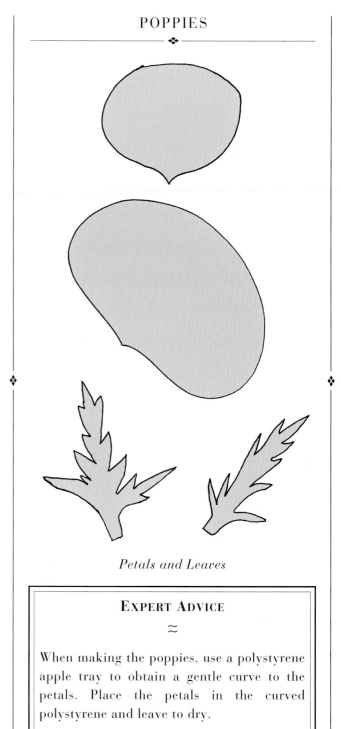

Petals and Leaves

EXPERT ADVICE

~

When making the poppies, use a polystyrene apple tray to obtain a gentle curve to the petals. Place the petals in the curved polystyrene and leave to dry.

~ 1 ~

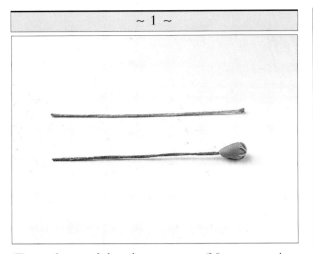

To make seed head, tape two 26-gauge wires together; hook one end. Make a small piece of green sugarpaste into a cone and place on the hooked end. Flatten top of cone slightly. With a pair of tweezers, pinch top of cone. Make black cotton stamens, see page 9.

~ 2 ~

Tape stamens beneath seed head. Paint tweezer lines black. Brush cotton ends with egg white; dip into black textured powder. Roll out red paste thinly, leaving a small centre ridge. Cut two small petals, ball edges, vein and place a 30-gauge wire in ridge. Leave to dry.

~ 3 ~

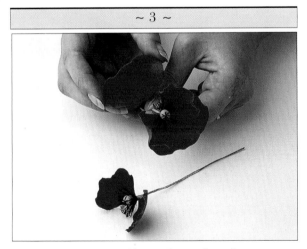

Tape the two small petals under the stamens opposite one another. Roll out red paste thinly and cut two large petals. Ball edges and vein as before. Place a little egg white on the bottom edges and stick opposite one another. Stand in a bottle to dry.

~ 4 ~

When dry, dust the flower with red powder. Paint in four black patches near the base of the stamens. Steam over a kettle. Leave to dry. Join leaves and buds at the middle of the flower stem.

MOTHER

25cm (10 in) teardrop cake
apricot glaze
1kg (2 lb) marzipan (almond paste)
1.25kg (2.5 lb) sugarpaste
clear alcohol (gin or vodka)
Royal Icing, see page 8
gold paint

EQUIPMENT

25 x 30cm (10 x 12 in) oral cake board
no. 1 and 42 piping tubes (tips)
small paintbrush
1m (1 yd) of 3mm (⅛ in) wide ribbon to
trim cake
1m (1 yd) of 15mm (⅝ in) wide ribbon to
trim board

FLOWERS

3 stems of bluebells, see page 27
4 bluebell leaves, see page 26
4 violets, see pages 28 – 29
16 violet leaves, see pages 11 – 13
2 wood anemones, see pages 28 – 29
6 sets of 3 wood anemone leaves,
see pages 11 – 13

Brush the cake with apricot glaze and cover with marzipan (almond paste). Allow to dry. Coat the board with sugarpaste and set aside. Brush the cake with clear alcohol and coat it with sugarpaste. When the paste is firm, place the cake on the board.

Trace the 'Mother' inscription below and scribe it onto the top of the cake. Using white royal icing and a no. 1 piping tube (tip), pipe the outline of the letters. Thin some icing to runout consistency and flood each letter shape with white icing. Place under a warm lamp to dry. When the runouts are completely dry, paint each letter with gold paint.

Using a no. 42 piping tube (tip), pipe a snail trail around the base of the cake. Place two lines of ribbon above this and secure with royal icing.

Make the flowers, see pages 27 – 29. Mould a piece of sugarpaste and make it into a small mound. Stick this on the board in the concave curve of the cake as a base in which to arrange the flowers.

Hide the sugarpaste under the flower arrangement with leaves and pebbles. Attach the ribbon to the board using double-sided tape.

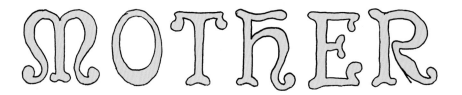

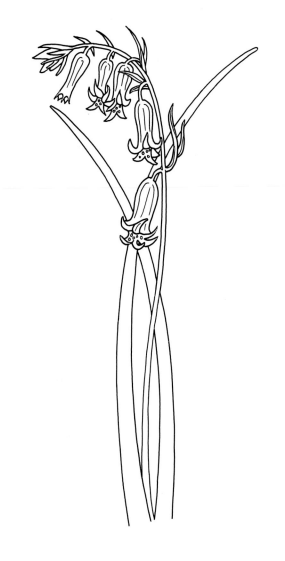

BLUEBELL LEAVES

Take a medium piece of green flower paste and roll it into a sausage. Thread a piece of 28-gauge wire into the paste and roll it gently between your hands so that the wire becomes embedded. Lay the wired paste on a non-stick board and squash it slightly with a palette knife, then use dowel rod to roll the paste on either side of the wire until it is quite thin. Use a pair of fine scissors to cut a long narrow leaf shape with the wire running down the centre of the paste. Gently stroke the edges of the leaf with a dogbone tool to thin them further and mark veins down the middle with a dresden tool. Leave to dry before dusting with colour.

~ 1 ~

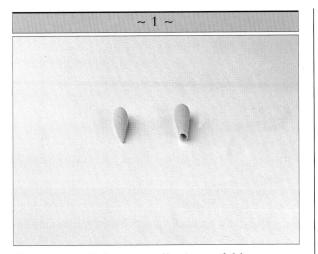

BLUEBELLS *Take a small piece of blue-mauve flower paste and roll into a narrow tapering cone. Insert a cocktail stick at the pointed end, push up about three quarters of the way and hollow out the cone into a tube, making sure that the edges are fine.*

~ 2 ~

Make six long cuts down the tube for petals. Cut the square corners from these petals and thin their edges with a cocktail stick, working on your index finger. Place the flower upside down on a piece of foam and gently stroke each petal towards the centre to curl inwards.

~ 3 ~

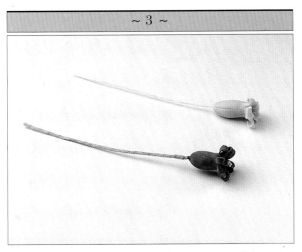

Make a hook in a piece of 30-gauge white wire and thread it through the middle and out the top of the flower. Extend the line of the petals by cutting down the length of the flower with a craft knife, making sure petals are well curled back. Add six fine stamens.

~ 4 ~

Make smaller pointed cones for buds. When dry, tape buds and flowers together, all on the same side of the stem. Dust flowers and stems lightly with blue-mauve dusting powder (petal dust/blossom tint). Add a tiny bract of blue paste at the base of each flower stem.

VIOLETS

Leaves

WOOD ANEMONES

Flower

Leaves

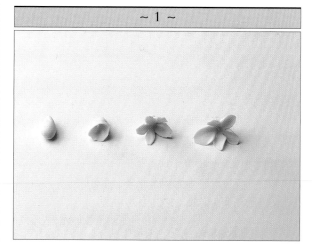

Shape a small piece of white flower paste into a cone. Hollow out the cone making sure the edges are thin. Make five fairly deep cuts to form petals: four should be the same size and one should be larger. Cut off the points on the corners of the petals with fine scissors.

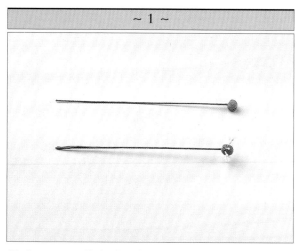

Take a small ball of light green flower paste and place it on the end of a piece of 30-gauge white wire. Push several small yellow stamens into the base of the ball. Leave to dry.

~ 2 ~

~ 3 ~

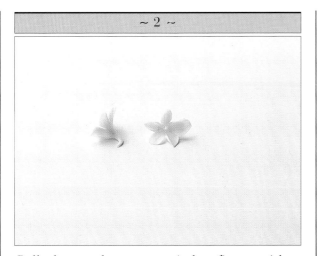

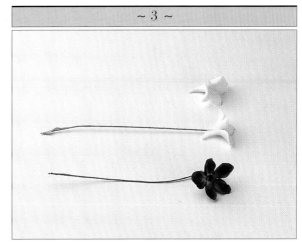

Roll the petals on your index finger with a cocktail stick to widen and slightly lengthen them, making sure the bottom petal remains larger than the others. Gently push the two top petals backwards, the middle two slightly inwards and the larger one slightly forwards.

Roll spur at back of flower between thumb and finger and curve gently upwards. Place orange stamen in throat of flower. Insert 28-gauge wire behind top petal. Leave to dry. Dust with violet dusting powder, leaving centre white. Bend wire over and down. Make leaves, see pages 11 – 13.

~ 2 ~

~ 3 ~

Roll out some white flower paste very thinly and cut out flower using a six-petal cutter, about 2cm (¾ in) diameter. Ball each petal with a dogbone tool and vein with a petal veiner or a piece of crêpe paper.

Cup the flower. Thread the wire with the stamens through centre. Secure with egg white; dry. Dust a stripe of burgundy down the back of each petal. Make leaves, see pages 11 – 13 and tape three sets to each single flower with white tape; dust stem burgundy.

HEATHER

20 x 15cm (8 x 6 in) oval cake
apricot glaze
1.25kg (2.5 lb) marzipan (almond paste)
1.25kg (2.5 lb) sugarpaste
clear alcohol (gin or vodka)
Royal Icing, see page 8
a selection of food colourings
EQUIPMENT
28 x 23cm (11 x 9 in) oval cake board
no. 1.5 piping tube (tip)
small paintbrushes
scriber
1m (1 yd) of 15mm (⅝ in) wide ribbon to
trim board
FLOWERS
6 stems of heather, see page 32

● Brush the cake with apricot glaze and cover with marzipan (almond paste). Allow to dry. Coat the board with sugarpaste and set aside. Brush the cake with clear alcohol and coat with sugarpaste. When the icing is firm, place the cake on the board. Leave to dry for 2 – 3 days.

● Trace the 'Happy Birthday' greeting, see page 70, and scribe it on the top of the cake. Paint the letters with food colouring. Trace and paint the landscape, see below, on the side of the cake, then allow to dry.

● Make the heather and arrange it in a small clump at the front of the cake. Make little pebbles to scatter underneath the heather, see page 10. Attach the ribbon to the board using double-sided tape.

Side Design

HEATHER

❖

Heather is a pretty flower which is easy to make but you need a lot of the flowers, which is time-consuming. It is nice to include a piece of heather in a bridal arrangement, as it is considered to be lucky.

Make the heather and leaves following the steps below, then tape the flowers together when dry. Cut a piece of 26-gauge wire and start taping the flowers at the top of the wire in small clusters. Tape the leaves underneath. Continue this process all the way down the wire, finishing with leaf clusters at the bottom.

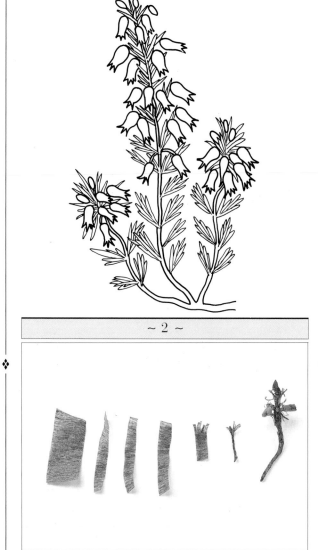

| ~ 1 ~ | ~ 2 ~ |

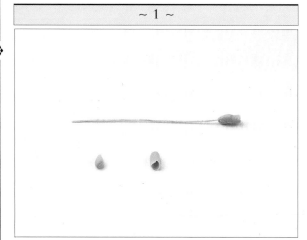

Cut several pieces of 33-gauge white wire, each approximately 10cm (4 in) in length. Make a cone with a very small piece of pink paste. Hollow the pointed end with a cocktail stick and thin the edges. With a cocktail stick, gently push the edges of the flower down slightly to make them uneven. Dip a piece of wire into egg white and pull it through the flower. Leave to dry. Make as many flowers as necessary.

Make the leaves by cutting several pieces of green florists' tape into 2.5cm (1 in) lengths. Cut each piece into three. Make a series of tiny cuts at the top of the tape and spread out the cuts, then roll the other end.

WILD STRAWBERRIES

25cm (10 in) trefoil cake
apricot glaze
1.25kg (2.5 lb) marzipan (almond paste)
1.5kg (3 lb) sugarpaste
clear alcohol (gin or vodka)
Royal Icing, see page 8
a selection of food colourings

EQUIPMENT

30cm (12 in) round cake board
no. 00 and 42 piping tubes (tips)
1m (1 yd) of 3mm (⅛ in) wide ribbon to trim cake
posy pick
1m (1 yd) of 15mm (⅝ in) wide ribbon to trim board

FLOWERS

17 wild strawberries, see page 34
11 wild strawberry flowers, see page 36
40 wild strawberry leaves, see pages 11 – 13

Brush the cake with apricot glaze and cover with marzipan (almond paste). Allow to dry. Coat the board with sugarpaste, then set aside. Brush the cake with clear alcohol and coat with sugarpaste. When the paste is firm, transfer the cake to the board.

Using a no. 42 piping tube (tip), pipe a snail trail around the base of the cake. Place a line of thin ribbon above this and secure it with royal icing.

Make the wild strawberries and flowers. Assemble the main plant spray and fix it in a posy pick in the centre of the cake.

For each of the smaller plants around the edge, take a small piece of sugarpaste and shape it into a neat mound. Stick one on the board in each indent of the cake, then use as holders for the small arrangements of strawberries. Conceal the paste using the larger leaves. Attach the ribbon to the board using double-sided tape.

Wild Strawberry Plant

~ 1 ~

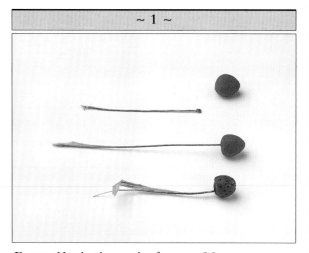

FRUIT Hook the end of some 26-gauge green wire. Roll red flower paste into a bulbous cone; dip the wire into egg white and insert into the base. Let dry. Using a no. 00 piping tube and brown royal icing, pipe tiny dots on the strawberry. Glaze with confectioners' glaze when dry.

WILD STRAWBERRY PLANTS

❖

An attractive little plant which is a suitable decoration on a cake for a man or woman and also very effective as a large, whole plant. The fruit may be modelled by hand or by using strawberry moulds, which are available commercially. Make the strawberries, flowers and leaves separately, then arrange the fruit, flowers and leaves in clusters.

~ 2 ~

Roll out some green paste very finely; make a calyx using a small calyx cutter. Soften the edges with a dogbone tool and vein lightly. Brush the top of the strawberry lightly with egg white, push the wire through the centre of the calyx and secure it on the fruit.

~ 3 ~

Tape the strawberries together, one beneath the other along a stem. A single stem can hold up to six fruits. Make the strawberry leaves, see pages 11 – 13.

~ 1 ~

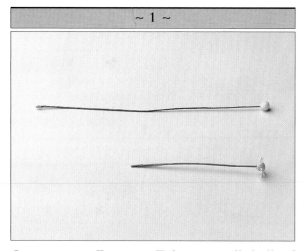

STRAWBERRY FLOWERS *Take a small ball of pale yellow flower paste and put it on the end of a 28-gauge light green wire. Push several small yellow stamens into the base. Leave to dry.*

~ 2 ~

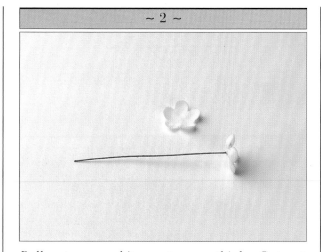

Roll out some white paste very thinly. Cut out the flower using a five-petal blossom cutter. Soften the edges of the petals and cup them using a dogbone tool. Attach the flower underneath the centre with a little egg white.

~ 3 ~

Roll out some light green paste and cut out the calyx shape. Soften the edges with a dogbone tool and secure it underneath the flower with a little egg white. Leave to dry. Assemble with fruit and leaves.

Strawberry Leaves

EASTER EGG CAKE

23cm (9 in) egg-shaped cake
apricot glaze
1kg (2 lb) marzipan (almond paste)
1.25kg (2.5 lb) sugarpaste
clear alcohol (gin or vodka)
Royal Icing, see page 8
a selection of food colourings
E Q U I P M E N T
20cm (8 in) round cake board
no. 42 piping tube (tip)
67cm (26 in) of 15mm (⅝ in) wide ribbon to
trim board
F L O W E R S
2 daffodils, see pages 38 and 41
3 daffodil leaves, see pages 11 – 13
5 primroses, see pages 38 and 40
14 primrose leaves, see pages 11 – 13
3 stems of pussy willow, see pages 42 – 43

● Brush the cake with apricot glaze and cover with marzipan (almond paste). Make sure the marzipan is smooth. Leave to dry for at least 24 hours.

● Coat the board with sugarpaste and leave to dry. Brush the marzipan with clear alcohol and apply the sugarpaste which must be 5mm-1cm (¼ – ½ in) thick. Smooth the paste by hand. This will take a little time – try to get the surface as smooth and flawless as possible. Leave to dry for at least 2 days.

● Position the cake towards the back of the board and secure with royal icing. Using a no. 42 piping tube (tip), pipe a shell pattern around the base of the cake.

● Trace the 'Easter' greeting, right, and scribe it slightly off centre on the side of the cake. Paint the letters with gold food colouring.

● Make the flowers. Form a piece of sugarpaste into a small mound to hold the flowers and arrange them in front of the egg. Hide the sugarpaste with the primrose leaves and little pebbles.

PRIMROSES

❖

Pretty flowers and easy to make, these are suitable for Easter and Mother's Day, as well as spring weddings or birthdays.

STAMPING OUT THE FLOWER SHAPE Shape a piece of pale yellow flower paste into a Mexican hat, making sure the point is quite slender. Place on the board and use a small rolling pin to roll the paste thin, from the point outwards. Cut out the shape using a primrose cutter, positioning it so that the point is in the centre of the cutter. Finish making the flower following the step-by-step instructions on page 40. Make the leaves following the instructions on pages 11 – 13.

EXPERT ADVICE

≈

Primroses have green or burgundy stems. If burgundy stems are required, use white wire and dust this with ruby-coloured dusting powder (petal dust/blossom tint) when the calyx is dry.

DAFFODILS

❖

There are several different varieties of daffodil, so choose the colour according to your requirements. Those described here are wild flowers and therefore they are pale yellow. Take two pieces of 24-gauge light green wire and tape them together. Attach four stamens to the top, leaving one of them slightly higher than the others. Brush these with egg white and then dip into yellow textured powder to give the impression of pollen.

Take a piece of pale yellow flower paste and make it into a Mexican hat shape, making sure the point is slender. Place on the board and use a small rolling pin to roll from the point outwards to make the paste thinner. Cut with a six-petal flower cutter, approximately 5cm (2 in) in diameter. Make the flower following the step-by-step instructions on page 41.

EXPERT ADVICE

≈

When making the trumpet of the flower, it is easier to join the edges if the paste is first placed around a piping tube (tip) for support.

~ 1 ~

PRIMROSE *Make a hole in the centre of the flower with a cone tool. With some cornflour on your index finger, gently roll each petal of the flower from the centre to the outside, to thin it down and widen it slightly. Gently stroke with a ball tool to cup the flower a little.*

~ 2 ~

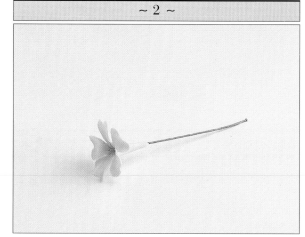

Take a piece of 26-gauge wire, dip it in egg white and pull through the centre of the flower. Insert a small green stamen into the centre. Leave to dry. When dry, paint the middle a darker yellow.

~ 3 ~

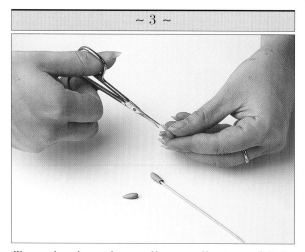

To make the calyx, roll a small piece of light green paste into a teardrop shape. With the sharp end of a cocktail stick, open up the pointed end of the paste and roll it on your index finger to hollow the cone. Cut out five 'V' shapes from the cone and roll each to thin out.

~ 4 ~

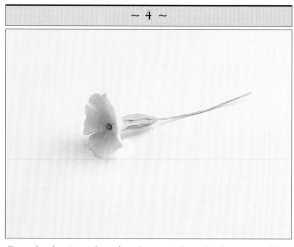

Brush the inside of calyx with a little egg white and slide it up wire. Position just below the top of the flower. Use tweezers to pinch a line up the middle of the points the full length of the calyx. When dry, assemble with leaves.

~ 1 ~

DAFFODIL *Make a hole in the centre of the flower using a cone-shaped tool. With a dogbone tool, soften and slightly stretch the petals; vein using a corn leaf veiner. Push three alternate petals inwards.*

~ 2 ~

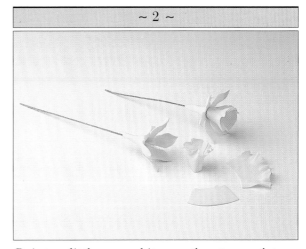

Paint a little egg white on the stamens' tape and pull through the centre of the daffodil. Cut out the trumpet shape; frill the outside edge. Join the two end edges, brush a little egg white in the centre of the flower and then place trumpet in the centre. Leave to dry.

~ 3 ~

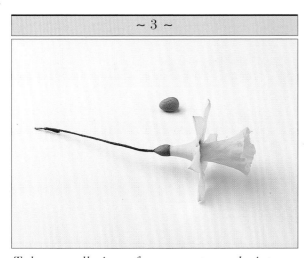

Take a small piece of green paste; make into an oval shape. Push this up the wire behind the back of the daffodil to form the seed pod.

~ 4 ~

Take a piece of white florists' tape. Cut the sheath and dust with cream powder; place behind the seed pod. Tape down the length of the wire with green tape; bend wire just behind sheath. Make leaves, see pages 11 – 13.

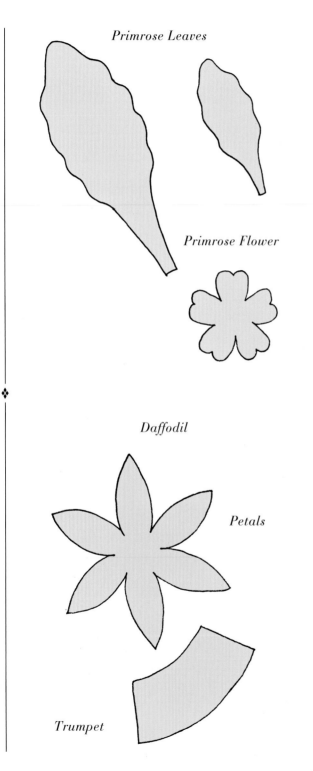

Primrose Leaves

Primrose Flower

Daffodil

Petals

Trumpet

PUSSY WILLOW

This is an easy plant to make and it looks very effective, as it adds height and contrast to arrangements of wild flowers. Begin by cutting a piece of 30-gauge white wire and making a small hook at one end. Shape a small piece of white flower paste into a cone, slightly elongated at one end. Dip the wire into egg white then place the cone on top of it. Make several of these in different sizes. Leave to dry overnight. To reproduce the furry silver down which grows on pussy willow, use white pollen granules or semolina mixed with silver dusting powder. Brush with egg white and dip into the pollen. Leave to dry.

For the yellow part of the pussy willow, brush a little egg white near the base, over the silver, and dip into yellow textured powder. As the pussy willow get smaller, the area of yellow decreases.

Follow the step-by-step instructions for completing the stems of pussy willow.

~ 1 ~

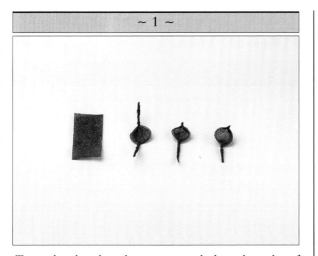

To make the sheath, cut several short lengths of brown, paper-type florists' tape. Twist each end of the tape leaving a small gap in the middle; cut off one end. Cup the flat piece of tape using a ball tool.

~ 2 ~

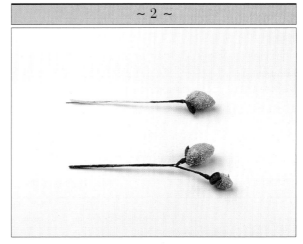

Tape one or two sheaths underneath each pussy willow. To assemble, take a piece of 26-gauge wire about 18cm (7 in) long; tape smallest bud in at top. Tape a little way down stem then add the next; tape close to stem. Continue to tape buds and sheaths in this manner.

~ 3 ~

As you go down the stem, the gap between the pussy willows should increase. Bend the twig away from each bud.

~ 4 ~

Dust the twig with a little brown or green dusting powder to make it look weathered.

CHRISTMAS STAR

15cm (6 in) star cake
apricot glaze
1kg (2 lb) marzipan (almond paste)
1kg (2 lb) Royal Icing, see page 8
a selection of food colourings
EQUIPMENT
25cm (10 in) round cake board
no. 00, 0, 1 and 1.5 piping tubes (tips)
side scraper
steel rule
1m (1 yd) of 3mm (⅛ in) wide ribbon to
trim cake
posy pick
1m (1 yd) of 15mm (⅝ in) wide ribbon to
trim board
FLOWERS
3 Christmas roses, see page 47
5 sets of 3 Christmas rose leaves, see pages
11 – 13
6 bunches of mistletoe, see page 46

● Brush the cake with apricot glaze and cover with marzipan (almond paste). Place the cake on the board. Coat the cake with white royal icing - ice the top first and leave to dry. Ice six alternate sides; leave to dry. When dry, ice the six remaining sides. Repeat this process three to five times until a smooth finish is achieved.

● When the cake is dry, using a no. 1.5 piping tube (tip), pipe a thin line around the edge of the board. Coat the board using runout icing. Leave to dry. Using a no. 1.5 piping tube (tip), pipe a snail trail around the base of the cake.

● Make a cardboard template of the pattern for the side of the cake, see below. Using a scriber, mark the pattern on the cake. Pipe the extension bridge using a no. 1 piping tube (tip), building it to approximately five lines deep. Leave until completely dry.

● When dry, soften a small amount of royal icing with a little water and, with a paintbrush, paint the icing over the inside of the bridge. This will neaten and strengthen it.

● Pipe in the extension lines using a no. 00 piping tube (tip). Pipe a line of small dots at the top of the extension work using a no. 0 piping tube (tip). Then continue with the same tube and pipe dots around the edges of the cake if liked.

● Make the flowers. Arrange the mistletoe in small bunches and place in the gaps, attaching with royal icing. Arrange the Christmas roses and foliage in a posy pick in the centre of the cake. Attach the ribbon to the board using double-sided tape.

Side Design

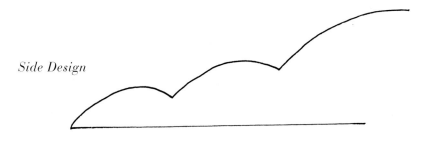

MISTLETOE

Roll a small piece of green-yellow paste into a thin cone. Dip a piece of 28-gauge wire into some egg white and insert it into the pointed end of the cone. Place on a board and roll with a small rolling pin to make a leaf which should curve slightly inwards. Vein the centre using a dresden tool. Repeat this process to make more leaves and leave to dry. Colour some white flower paste with a tiny drop of yellow. Make the berries by rolling small balls of paste 5mm – 1cm (¼ – ½ in) long. Place each one on a 28-gauge hooked wire. Leave to dry.

When everything is dry, dust the leaves with light green dusting powder. Paint a tiny cross pattern on top of the mistletoe berry with very dark brown and leave to dry. Glaze the berries with white vegetable fat (shortening) and assemble as shown in the close-up photograph. Make a tiny cone of green paste and place in the middle of each pair of leaves.

~ 1 ~

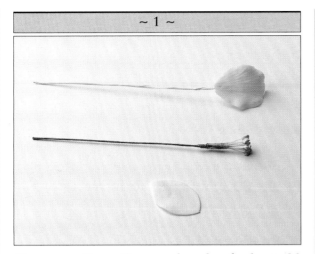

CHRISMAS ROSE *Tape a bunch of about 30 stamens onto 26-gauge wire. Roll out white sugarpaste, leaving a small ridge for wire and cut out a petal. Insert a piece of 30-gauge white wire in the ridge. Vein using a corn leaf veiner and soften edges with a dogbone tool.*

~ 2 ~

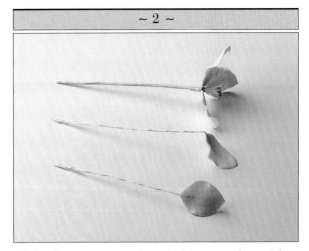

Make five more petals and leave to dry with a slight curve. When dry, arrange them around the stamens using white tape.

~ 3 ~

Make tiny cones of green paste, hollow with a cocktail stick and place at base of the stamens. Dust the flower centre bright green. If making sepals, attach these underneath petals. Tape down the wire. Dust the stem with burgundy. Make leaves, see pages 11 – 13.

~ 4 ~

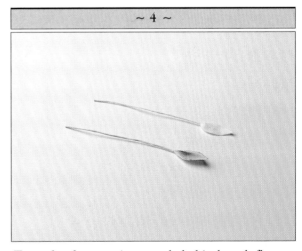

To make the two tiny sepals behind each flower, follow the instructions for petals but cut spear shapes instead of petal shapes. Dust with light green and burgundy powder.

BETHANY

20cm (8 in) scalloped oval cake
apricot glaze
1kg (2 lb) marzipan (almond paste)
1.25kg (2.5 lb) sugarpaste
clear alcohol (gin or vodka)
Royal Icing, see page 8
a selection of food colourings

EQUIPMENT

25cm (10 in) scalloped oval cake board
no. 1 and 42 icing tubes (tips)
dog rose stencil
67cm (26 in) of 3mm (⅛ in) wide ribbon to
trim cake
1m (1 yd) of 15mm (⅝ in) wide ribbon to
trim board

FLOWERS

4 dog roses, see pages 50 – 51
29 dog rose leaves, see pages 11 – 13

● Brush the cake with apricot glaze and cover with marzipan (almond paste). Allow to dry. Coat the board with sugarpaste and set aside. Brush the cake with clear alcohol; coat with sugarpaste. When the icing is firm, transfer the cake to the board.

● Trace the name inscription and scribe it onto the top of the cake. Using white royal icing and a no. 1 piping tube (tip), pipe the outline of the letters. With pink runout icing, flood each letter, then place under a warm lamp to dry.

● Using a no. 42 piping tube (tip), pipe a snail trail around the base of the cake. Secure thin ribbon with royal icing around the cake above the snail trail.

● Use a dog rose stencil to apply the decoration on the side of the cake. The stencil design is also shown below. Lay the stencil flat on the cake, then spread some royal icing over it. Lift the stencil away cleanly and leave the royal icing to dry. Paint the design with food colouring when the icing has dried thoroughly.

● Make the flowers. Assemble the roses in a natural-looking arrangement and secure on the cake with royal icing. Place a single flower and leaves on the board in one of the scallops around the cake side. Attach the ribbon to the board using double-sided tape.

EXPERT ADVICE

≈

For an open flower, pierce a hole in the bottom of the cup of a polystyrene apple tray and push the wire from the flower down through the hole, then leave to dry. To make a flower that is just opening, either put tiny pieces of sponge under the petals or hang the flower upside down to dry.

Side Design

DOG ROSE

❖

Dog roses come in pale pink or white, so choose the colour according to your cake design.

Start by making the centre of the flower, using cotton for the stamens, see page 9. Tape the stamens to a piece of 26-gauge wire and trim the cottons to about 5mm (¼ in) in length. Splay the cottons, leaving a gap in the centre, and brush their ends with egg white. Then dip them in a golden-coloured pollen dust. Shape a tiny piece of green flower paste into a cone. Brush egg white on the bulbous end of the cone and stick it in the centre of the stamens. Set aside.

To make the flower, take a medium-sized piece of white flower paste and shape it into a Mexican hat. Roll the paste from the centre to the outside to make it thinner. Cut the flower shape using a large primrose or dog rose cutter placed over the Mexican hat of paste, with the point in the middle. Make a hole in the centre of the flower with the point of a dowel rod. Follow the instructions opposite to finish the flower.

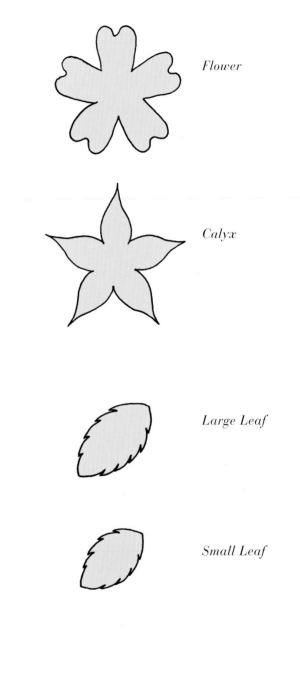

Flower

Calyx

Large Leaf

Small Leaf

EXPERT ADVICE

≈

When dusting the dog rose with colour, to avoid brushing pink on the centre of the flower, hold it at an angle so that the excess dusting powder (petal dust/blossom tint) falls away from the centre of the flower.

~ 1 ~

Roll each petal on your index finger using a cocktail stick, working from the centre of the heart shape outwards. This will both widen and thin the petals. Cup and shape the petals gently with a dogbone tool.

~ 2 ~

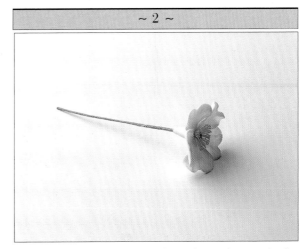

Brush a little egg white directly underneath the stamens. With the flower in your left hand, gently push the wire through the centre. Pull the stamens down to cover the florists' tape. Leave to dry.

~ 3 ~

To make the calyx, take a medium piece of light green paste, roll it out flat and cut out using a calyx cutter. Make tiny cuts around the edge of the calyx and soften the edges with a dogbone tool. Attach the calyx underneath the flower with a little egg white.

~ 4 ~

Shape another small piece of paste into an oval shape. Push this up the wire underneath the calyx. Make leaves, see pages 11 – 13. When everything is dry, dust the rose with pale pink dusting powder (petal dust/blossom tint), from the outside towards the centre.

HEDGEROW

15cm (6 in) square cake
apricot glaze
1kg (2 lb) marzipan (almond paste)
1.25kg (2.5 lb) sugarpaste
clear alcohol (gin or vodka)
Royal Icing, see page 8
a selection of food colourings

EQUIPMENT

23cm (9 in) square cake board
no. 0, 1, 1.5 and 42 piping tubes (tips)
honeysuckle stencil
posy pick
scriber
68cm (27 in) of 3mm (⅛ in) wide ribbon to
trim cake
1m (1 yd) of 15mm (⅝ in) wide ribbon to
trim board

FLOWERS

8 blackberries, see page 54
12 blackberry leaves, see pages 11 – 13
8 honeysuckle flowers, see page 55
8 honeysuckle buds, see page 55

● Brush the cake with apricot glaze and cover with marzipan (almond paste). Allow to dry. Coat the board with sugarpaste and set aside. Brush the cake with clear alcohol and coat with sugarpaste. When the paste is firm, place the cake on the board. Pipe a snail trail around the base of the cake using a no. 42 piping tube (tip).

● Make a card template of the corner pattern, see page 70 – only one-third need be drawn. Place the template in position and scribe around it, so that all three sections for a single corner are scribed and they each join.

● Use a no. 0 piping tube (tip) to pipe the cornelli work, piping just inside the scribed line. Repeat this process for the three remaining corners. Take a no. 1.5 piping tube (tip) and pipe over the scribed line. Use a no. 1 piping tube (tip) to pipe another line immediately on top of the first. Pipe a third, final line, using a no. 0 piping tube (tip).

● Use a honeysuckle stencil to apply the design to the side of the cake. The design for the stencil is also shown below. Lay the stencil flat on the cake, then spread some royal icing over it. Lift the stencil away cleanly. Leave to dry. Paint the design with food colouring.

● Make the flowers. Arrange the flowers together in a posy. Place a posy pick in the middle of the cake and put the flowers in the pick. Attach the ribbon to the board using double-sided tape.

Honeysuckle Side Design

BLACKBERRIES

To make the blackberries, take a piece of 26-gauge wire and form a hook at one end. Start by shaping a piece of black flower paste into a cone and place this on the wire. Leave to dry.

EXPERT ADVICE

≈

To make a ripening fruit, colour small balls of paste a deep claret and assemble them among the other black balls so that the fruit is a mixture of both colours.

Bramble Leaves

Blackberry Calyx

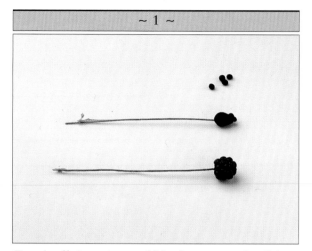

~ 1 ~

Break off tiny pieces of black paste and roll into balls. Brush egg white onto the cone and stick the balls of paste to it. Leave to dry. When dry, dip into confectioners' glaze. Leave to dry overnight.

~ 2 ~

To make the calyx, roll out some green paste. Using a very small calyx cutter, cut the shape. Gently soften the edges slightly with a dogbone tool. Attach the calyx underneath the fruit with a little egg white. Make leaves, see pages 11 – 13.

HONEYSUCKLE

Start by making the buds. They come in several different sizes ranging from about 5mm – 2.5cm (¼ – 1 in). Make a hook in a piece of 28-gauge wire. Shape some pale cream flower paste into a slender teardrop. Thread the pointed end of the paste onto the wire. Slightly curve the bud upwards and make five long cuts lengthways. Leave to dry. Honeysuckle varies in colour so dust accordingly.

Tape six mini stamens to a 28-gauge wire and leave one standing proud of the others. Shape a piece of cream paste into a Mexican hat. Use a honeysuckle cutter to cut the flower shape. Make a hole in the centre. Soften the petals and tongue with a cocktail stick (toothpick).

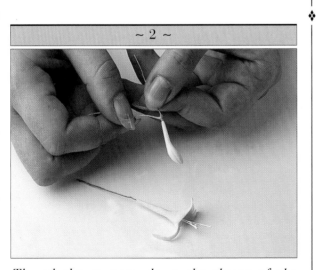

Thread the stamens down the throat of the flower, leaving them proud. Roll the back of the flower between your thumb and forefinger to form a slender back. Leave to dry. Wrap a thin piece of florists' tape below the flowers and buds to make the calyx.

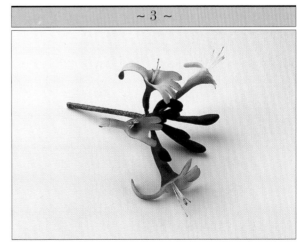

Dust flowers and buds as required. Arrange the buds in a ring, with the flowers in a ring directly underneath.

AUTUMN

20 x 13cm (8 x 5 in) octagonal cake
apricot glaze
1.25kg (2.5 lb) marzipan (almond paste)
clear alcohol (gin or vodka)
1.5kg (3 lb) sugarpaste
Royal Icing, see page 8
a selection of food colourings
gold paint

EQUIPMENT

20 x 30cm (12 x 8 in) octagonal cake board
no. 1.5 and 42 piping tubes (tips)
0.75m (¾ yd) of 3mm (⅛ in) wide ribbon to
trim cake
1m (1 yd) of 15mm (⅝ in) wide ribbon to
trim board

FLOWERS

6 hazelnuts, see page 58
8 hazelnut leaves, see pages 11 – 13
12 white bryony berries, see page 59
6 white bryony leaves, see pages 11 – 13

● Brush the cake with apricot glaze and cover with marzipan (almond paste). Brush the marzipan-coated cake with clear alcohol and coat with sugarpaste. Coat the board with sugarpaste and set aside. When the paste is firm, place the cake on the board.

● Using a no. 42 piping tube (tip), pipe a snail trail around the base of the cake. Place two lines of thin ribbon above this, secured with royal icing.

● Trace a greeting, as required or as shown below, and scribe it onto the top of the cake. Pipe over this using a little white royal icing and a no. 1.5 piping tube (tip). When dry, paint over the letters using gold paint.

● Make the flowers. Arrange the bryony and the hazelnuts together, then secure the sprays on the cake with royal icing. Place two leaves and two hazelnuts on the board, securing with royal icing. Attach the ribbon to the board using double-sided tape.

on your Retirement

HAZELNUTS

❖

Hazelnuts look very effective and are quick and easy to make.

Start by colouring some flower paste in light green or light brown. Take a piece of 24-gauge wire and make a hook in it at one end. Shape a piece of light brown paste into a cone, then form it into a hazelnut shape. Place the hooked end of the wire in the flat end of the cone and leave to dry overnight.

ASSEMBLING THE ARRANGEMENT

❖

When all the individual pieces are dry and coloured, bend the nuts at an angle and tape them close together in bunches of three to five, taping in leaves as required.

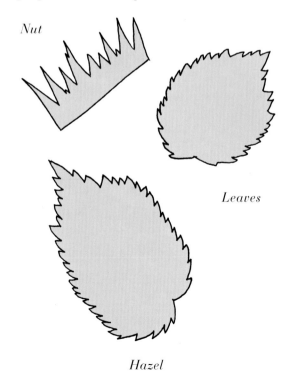

Nut

Leaves

Hazel

~ 1 ~

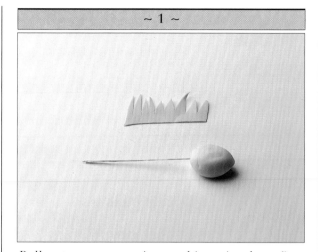

Roll out green paste into a thin strip about 5cm (2 in) long and 1cm (½ in) wide. Cut the top of the paste into an uneven zig-zag pattern, then thin down each point with a cocktail stick (toothpick). Make sure points do not get too rounded, if they do trim with scissors.

~ 2 ~

Brush egg white on the straight edge of paste and wrap around nut base. Turn down some points; dry. Dust the nut pale brown and husk green-brown. Make husk's tips darker brown. Varnish nut with half-strength confectioners' glaze. Make leaves, see pages 11 – 13.

WHITE BRYONY

I have chosen bryony as it grows later in the year, once the flowers have finished, when the colours of the berries and leaves are at their most eye-catching.

Follow the steps, right, for making the berries and leaves. Start by colouring some flower paste cream, red, orange and yellow, then make the berries. Make the leaves before assembling the stems. The berries are taped together in small clusters once they are dry. To assemble the stems, starting from the top, tape down the stem using the small leaves first, then add the tendrils, berries and other leaves.

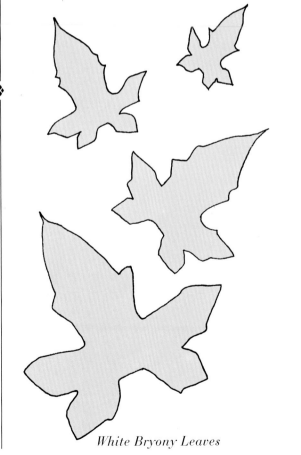

White Bryony Leaves

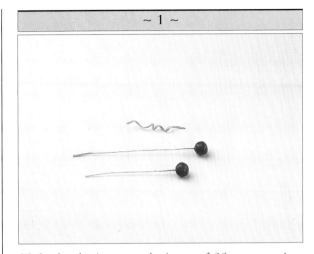

~ 1 ~

Make hooks in several pieces of 33-gauge wire. Roll small balls of red, orange and yellow paste. Dip the hooked ends of the wire into egg white and place the balls on them. Leave to dry. Dust with a corresponding colour. Glaze with confectioners' glaze.

~ 2 ~

For leaves, see pages 11 – 13; dust golden-brown and steam them. Take a piece of white florists' tape about 10cm (4 in) long and cut into four. Roll these into needle shapes; wind around cocktail sticks (toothpicks) or a paint-brush to make tendrils. Dust golden-brown.

PERIWINKLE

15cm (6 in) heart cake
apricot glaze
1kg (2 lb) marzipan (almond paste)
1.25kg (2.5 lb) sugarpaste
Royal Icing, see page 8
a selection of food colourings
EQUIPMENT
23cm (9 in) heart cake board
no. 1.5 and 42 piping tubes (tips)
Garrett frill cutter
cocktail stick (toothpick)
61cm (24 in) of 3mm (⅛ in) wide ribbon to
trim cake
1m (1 yd) of 15mm (⅝ in) wide ribbon to
trim board
FLOWERS
2 periwinkle flowers, see pages 62 – 63
4 periwinkle buds, see page 63
18 periwinkle leaves, see pages 11 – 13

Brush the cake with apricot glaze and cover with marzipan (almond paste). Allow to dry. Coat the board with sugarpaste and set aside. Brush the cake with clear alcohol and coat with sugarpaste. When the paste is firm, transfer the cake to the board.

Measure the circumference of the cake. Make a greaseproof paper (parchment) template to fit the side of the cake and fold it into equal sections. Draw a slight curve across the folded section of paper – this will be used as a guide for attaching the frill. Open out the paper and secure it around the cake. Scribe the curves onto the cake through the paper, following the drawn line. Remove the template.

Pipe a snail trail around the base of the cake using a no. 42 piping tube (tip). Leave to dry.

Make a double Garrett frill using white and lilac sugarpaste. Attach the frill to the scribed lines on the cake using egg white. Gently lift the edge of the frill with a soft brush. Neaten the top edge with a small dot pattern using a no. 1.5 piping tube (tip) and white royal icing.

Cut short lengths of the narrow ribbon and tie neat bows, making one for the top of each curve. Attach the bows to the cake with a little royal icing.

Make the flowers and arrange them in a natural-looking spray. Secure the spray to the cake with royal icing. Attach the ribbon to the board using double-sided tape.

EXPERT ADVICE

≈

A clean, uncluttered cake design provides the perfect backdrop for the strong shape and colour of the periwinkle spray. Variegated leaves may be made instead of the plain green ones shown, if preferred, see instructions on page 63.

BIRDSFOOT TREFOIL

❖

For this plant you need several flowers and even more leaves but it is worth the effort for it is very pretty. Start by cutting a piece of 36-gauge scientific wire and make a hook in one end. Mould a tiny piece of yellow paste into a teardrop shape and attach it to the wire. Allow to dry. Continue building up the flowers, following step-by-step instructions on page 68.

Flower   *Leaves*

Birdsfoot Trefoil Plant

SCABIOUS

❖

This well-known pastel-coloured flower blooms between July and September, so it is suitable for use on a summer wedding cake. Start by making the calyx. Take three lengths of 28-gauge wire and tape them together leaving about 5mm (¼ in) free at the top. Open out the free ends of the wire. Using a small daisy cutter, cut two shapes from light green paste. Brush egg white on one and place it on top of the wires. Thread the other one up the wire and attach it underneath the top piece, turning it so the points alternate and do not align directly beneath each other. Hang upside down to dry. Colour some flower paste a blue-mauve colour. Follow the step-by-step instructions opposite to make the flowers.

Calyx

Leaves

~ 1 ~

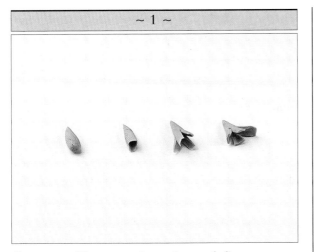

SCABIOUS Shape a tiny piece of flower paste into a cone and hollow it out slightly. Make four long even cuts down the length of the cone for petals and splay these out. Trim three of the petals.

~ 2 ~

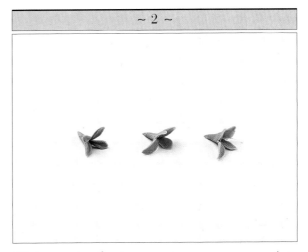

With a pair of scissors cut away corner points from the petals. Roll each petal with a cocktail stick and cup the three short ones with a glass-headed pin. Place a tiny stamen in the centre of the flower.

~ 3 ~

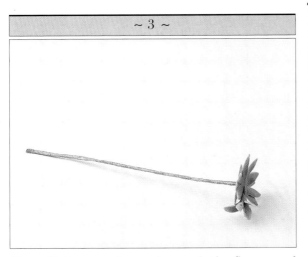

Put a little gum glue underneath the flower and attach it to the edge of the calyx. The part of the flower with the long lip should be hanging downwards. Continue making the flowers and assembling them around the outer edge.

~ 4 ~

The inner flowers are made in the same way but they are smaller and they do not have the long lips. Place some more gum glue in the middle of the flower and continue working around until the centre has been filled. Make leaves, see pages 11 – 13.

~ 1 ~

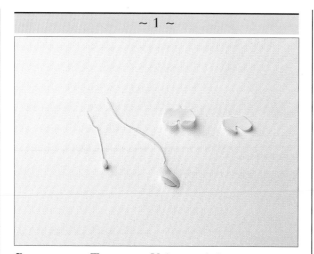

BIRDSFOOT TREFOIL *Using mini sweet pea cutters, cut the wings of the trefoil. Elongate slightly and thin edges. Place on sponge and ball slightly to curve petals inwards. Mark a crease in centre and place behind teardrop shape. For an open flower, pull the petals back.*

~ 2 ~

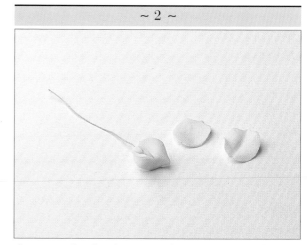

Cut out the back petal of the flower using the second cutter. Thin down the edges and mark a crease down the middle. Brush a little egg white near the base of the petal. Place behind the wings and pull backwards.

~ 3 ~

Make the calyx by taking a tiny piece of pale green flower paste. Make a cone shape, hollow this out with a cocktail stick and cut five tiny 'V' shapes out of the top. Push the calyx up the wire and secure behind flower with a little egg white.

~ 4 ~

When the flowers are dry, dust with yellow and a little red dusting powder (petal dust/blossom tint). Assemble in groups of four to five flowers. Make leaves, see pages 11 – 13. Assemble leaves in pairs or threes. Follow the diagram on pages 11 – 13 to help with assembly.

All leaves use Christmas green, dusted with a selection of green powders, such as holly/ivy, leaf, moss and forest, depending on the depth of colour required.

Acorns, Oak Apples and Oak Leaves
Paste Colour: cream.
Dusting Powder: brown, bulrush, chestnut and cream.

Birdsfoot Trefoil
Paste Colour: daffodil.
Dusting Powder: sunflower.

Blackberries
Paste Colour: black.
Dusting Powder: claret.

Bluebells
Paste Colour: mixed bluebell and lilac.
Dusting Powder: mixed bluebell and lavender.

Bryony Leaves
Paste Colour: cream.
Dusting Powder: chestnut and bulrush.

Bryony Berries
Paste Colour: red compound, sunflower and tangerine.
Dusting Powder: red, sunflower and tangerine.

Chestnut Leaves and Conkers
Paste Colour: cream and paprika.
Dusting Powder: brown, bulrush, chestnut, black, sunflower and skintone.

Christmas Rose
Paste Colour: white.
Dusting Powder: cyclamen and leaf green.

Daffodil
Paste Colour: daffodil.
Dusting Powder: mixed primrose and white.

Dog Rose
Paste Colour: white.
Dusting Powder: pastel pink.

Hazelnuts and Leaves
Paste Colour: cream.

Dusting Powder: chestnut and bulrush.

Heather
Paste Colour: rose.
Dusting Powder: rose.

Honeysuckle
Paste Colour: cream.
Dusting Powder: cyclamen and thrift.

Mistletoe
Paste Colour: Christmas green.
Dusting Powder: leaf green.

Oats
Paste Colour: cream.
Dusting Powder: cream.

Periwinkle
Paste Colour: white.
Dusting Powder: mixed cornflower, plum and lavender.

Poppies
Paste Colour: red compound.
Dusting Powder: red.

Primrose
Paste Colour: daffodil.
Dusting Powder: mixed primrose and white.

Pussy Willow
Paste Colour: white.
Dusting Powder: silver.

Scabious
Paste Colour: mixed lilac and bluebell.
Dusting Powder: mixed lavender and cornflower.

Violets
Paste Colour: white.
Dusting Powder: mixed cornflower and plum.

Wild Strawberries
Paste Colour: red compound.
Dusting Powder: red.

Wood Anemone
Paste Colour: white.
Dusting Powder: cyclamen.

Harvest Cake, see page 20

Happy Birthday

Heather, see page 30

Christmas Star:
Petal and Leaves for
Christmas Rose, see page 44

Hedgerow:
Corner Side and Top
Design, see page 52

Teardrop Cakes
Enlarge to 135 per cent on a photocopier

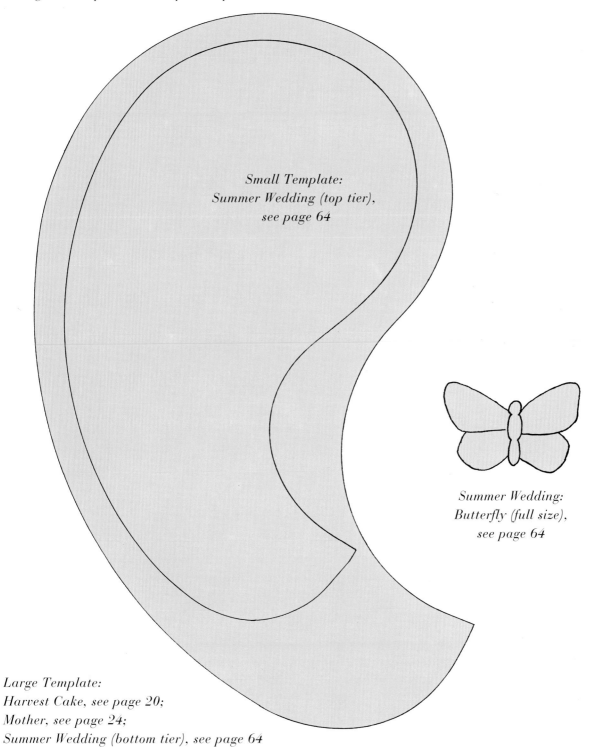

Small Template:
Summer Wedding (top tier),
see page 64

Summer Wedding:
Butterfly (full size),
see page 64

Large Template:
Harvest Cake, see page 20;
Mother, see page 24;
Summer Wedding (bottom tier), see page 64

INDEX

FOR FURTHER INFORMATION

Merehurst is the leading publisher of cake decorating books and has an excellent range of titles to suit cake decorators of all levels. Please send for a free catalogue, stating the title of this book:

United Kingdom
Marketing Department
Merehurst Ltd.
Ferry House
51 – 57 Lacy Road
London SW15 1PR
Tel: 0181 780 1177
Fax: 0181 780 1714

U.S.A./Canada
Foxwood International Ltd.
150 Nipissing Road # 6
Milton
Ontario L9T 5B2
Canada
Tel: 0101 905 875 4040
Fax: 0101 905 875 1668

Australia
Herron Book Distributors
91 Main Street
Kangaroo Point
Queensland 4169
Australia
Tel: 010 61 7 891 2866
Fax: 010 61 7 891 2909

Other Territories
For further information
contact:
International Sales
Department at United
Kingdom address.